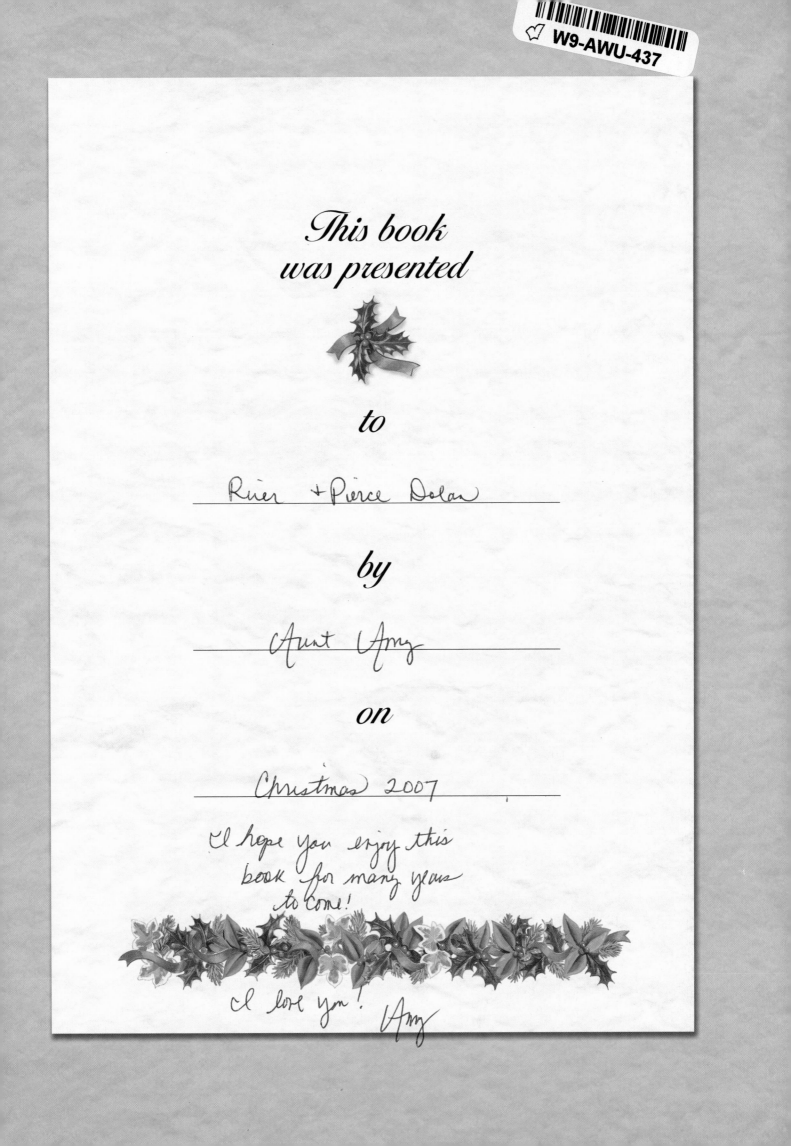

*This book
was presented*

to

River + Pierce Dolan

by

Aunt Amy

on

Christmas 2007

I hope you enjoy this
book for many years
to come!

I love you!

Amy

My Favorite
Christmas Songs

Designed by Tatia M. Lockridge
All arrangements created and written by Justin Peters for Justin Peters Music.

ISBN: 1-40372-546-5
15400 My Favorite Christmas Songs
Printed in the U.S.A.

06 07 08 LBM 10 9 8 7 6 5 4 3 2 1

My Favorite
Christmas Songs

Over the river

and through the woods

To have a full day of play.

The bells are ringing

"Ting-a-ling,"

For this is Christmas Day!

My Favorite Christmas Songs

Illustrated by Ruth Palmer

Dalmatian Press

Jingle Bells

Words and Music: James Pierpoint, 1857

as arranged by Justin Peters

Up on the Housetop

Words and Music: Benjamin R. Hanby

as arranged by Justin Peters

Up on the house - top, rein - deer pause;
First comes the stock - ing of lit - tle Nell.
Next comes the stock - ing of lit - tle Will.

Out jumps good ol' San - ta Claus!
Oh, dear San - ta, fill it well.
Oh, just see what a glo - rious fill!

Down through the chim - ney with lots of toys, All for the lit - tle ones'
Give her a dol - ly that laughs and cries; One that will o - pen and
Here is a ham - mer and lots of tacks; Al - so a ball and a

Christ - mas joys! Ho, ho, ho! Who wouldn't go?
shut her eyes.
whip that cracks!

Ho, ho, ho! Who would-n't go_____ Up on the house - top,

click, click, click! Down through the chim - ney with ol' Saint Nick!

And suddenly there was

with the angel a multitude

of the heavenly host

praising God and saying:

"Glory to God in the highest,

and on earth peace,

goodwill toward men!"

—Luke 2:13, 14

Hark! the Herald Angels Sing

Words: Charles Wesley, 1739

Music: Felix Mendelssohn, 1840
as arranged by Justin Peters

I Saw Three Ships

Words and Music: William Sandys, 1833

as arranged by Justin Peters

I saw three ships come sail - ing in on
And what was in those ships all three, on
'Twas Ma - ry, Jo - seph, and the Babe, on

Christ - mas Day, on Christ - mas Day. I
Christ - mas Day, on Christ - mas Day? And
Christ - mas Day, on Christ - mas Day. 'Twas

saw three ships come sail - ing in on
what was in those ships all three, on
Ma - ry, Jo - seph, and the Babe, on

Christ - mas Day in the morn - ing.
Christ - mas Day in the morn - ing?
Christ - mas Day in the morn - ing.

Deck the Halls

Traditional Welsh Carol

as arranged by Justin Peters

Deck the halls with boughs of hol-ly! Fa la la la la, la la la la.
See the blaz-ing Yule be-fore us. Fa la la la la, la la la la.
Fast a-way the old year pas-ses. Fa la la la la, la la la la.

'Tis the sea-son to be jol-ly. Fa la la la la, la la la la
Strike the harp and join the chor-us! Fa la la la la, la la la la
Hail the new, ye lads and las-ses. Fa la la la la, la la la la

Don we now our gay ap-pa-rel. Fa la la, la la la, la la la
Fol-low me in mer-ry meas-ure, Fa la la, la la la, la la la
Sing we joy-ous all to-geth-er, Fa la la, la la la, la la la

Troll the an-cient Yule-tide ca-rol. Fa la la la la, la la la la
While I tell of Yule-tide treas-ure. Fa la la la la, la la la la
Heed-less of the wind and weath-er. Fa la la la la, la la la la

His eyes—how they twinkled!

His dimples—how merry!

His cheeks were like roses,

his nose like a cherry!

His droll little mouth

was drawn up like a bow,

And the beard of his chin

was as white as the snow.

—*Clement Clarke Moore*

Jolly Old Saint Nicholas

Words and Music: Anonymous
often attributed to Benjamin R. Hanby

as arranged by Justin Peters

We Wish You a Merry Christmas

English Traditional

as arranged by Justin Peters

Joy to the World

On the twelfth day of Christmas

my true love gave to me:

Twelve drummers drumming

Eleven pipers piping

Ten lords a-leaping

Nine ladies dancing

Eight maids a-milking

Seven swans a-swimming

Six geese a-laying

Five golden rings

Four calling birds

Three French hens

Two turtledoves

and a partridge in a pear tree!

O Christmas Tree (O Tannenbaum)

Traditional German Carol

as arranged by Justin Peters

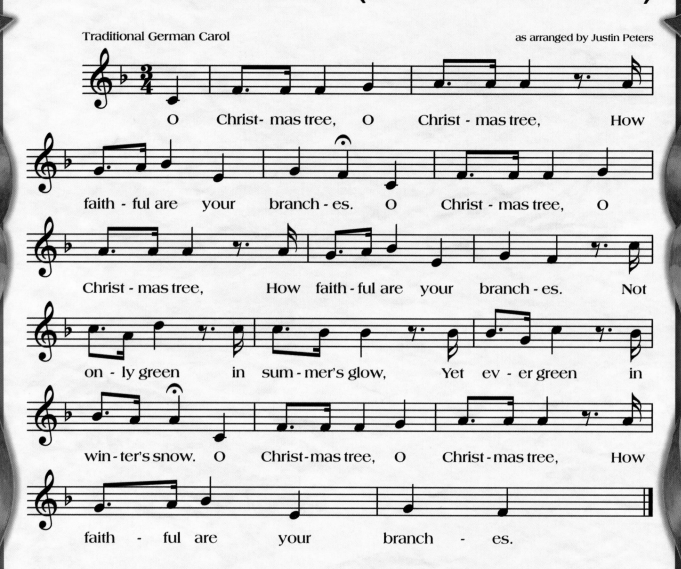

O Christmas tree, O Christmas tree,
You stand so fair and lovely.
O Christmas tree, O Christmas tree,
You stand so fair and lovely.
Your silver star, so pure and bright,
Reflects each tiny candle's light.
O Christmas tree, O Christmas tree,
You stand so fair and lovely.

German:
O Tannenbaum, O Tannenbaum,
Wie treu sind deine Blätter.
O Tannenbaum, O Tannenbaum,
Wie treu sind deine Blätter.

O Christmas tree, O Christmas tree,
You bear a wondrous message.
O Christmas tree, O Christmas tree,
You bear a wondrous message.
You bid us true and faithful be,
And trust in God unchangingly.
O Christmas tree, O Christmas tree,
You bear a wondrous message.

Du grünst nicht nur zur Sommerzeit,
Nein auch in Winter wenn es schneit.
O Tannenbaum, O Tannenbaum,
Wie treu sind deine Blätter.

Away in a Manger

Verses 1 & 2: Anonymous
Verse 3: John T. McFarland

Music: James Murray
as arranged by Justin Peters

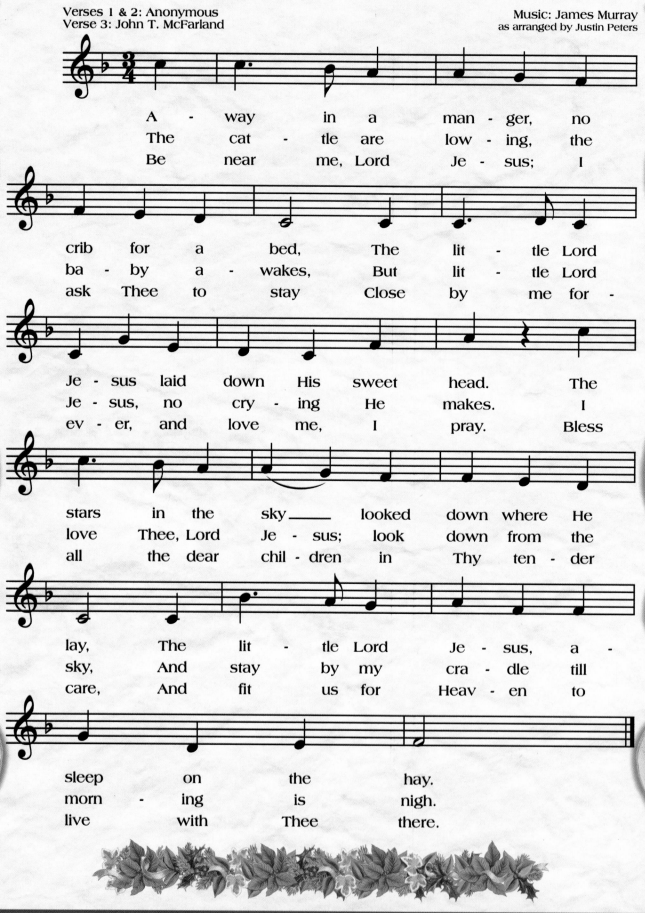

There's a song in the air!

There's a star in the sky!

There's a mother's deep prayer

and a baby's low cry!

And the star rains its fire

while the beautiful sing,

For the manger of Bethlehem

cradles a King.

—*Josiah G. Holland*